D1470341

BAD
TO THE
BONE

BAD
TO THE
BONE

Celebrating GOOD TIMES and BAD BEHAVIOR!

WILLOW CREEK PRESS

Published by Willow Creek Press
P.O. Box 147
Minocqua, Wisconsin 54548
Design: Donnie Rubo

Photo credits: p2 © Renee Stockdale/AnimalsAnimals; p6 © Jean M. Fogle; p9 © John Daniels/Ardea London; p13 © J. & P. Wegner/AnimalsAnimals; p14 © Daniel Johnson/Norvia Behling; p17 © Renee Stockdale/AnimalsAnimals; p18 © Lee Thomas Kjos; p21 © Jean M. Fogle; p25 © Daniel Johnson/Norvia Behling; p29 © DusanSmetana.com; p30 © Chris Harvey/Ardea London; p34 © Cheryl A. Ertelt; p37 © Frank S. Balthis; p38 © Renee Stockdale/AnimalsAnimals; p41 © Norvia Behling; p42 © Jean Higgines/Unicorn Stock Photos; p46 © Chris Harvey/Ardea London; p49 © Isabelle Francais; p50 Cheryl A. Ertelt; p53,54 © Frank S. Balthis; p57 © Bonnie Nance; p58 © Cheryl A. Ertelt; p61 © Eric R. Berndt/Unicorn Stock Photos; p62 © Renee Stockdale/AnimalsAnimals; p65 © Bonnie Nance; p66 © Jean M. Fogle; p69 © Norvia Behling; p70 © Cheryl A. Ertelt; p73 © Norvia Behling; p74 © Thomas Dressler/Ardea London; p78 © Norvia Behling; p80,81 © Jean M. Fogle; p82 © Renee Stockdale/AnimalsAnimals; p85 © Johan DeMeester/Ardea London; p86 © Frank S. Balthis; p89 © Norvia Behling; p90 © Ron Kimball/ronkimballstock.com; p93 © Bonnie Nance; p94 © Kent Dannen; p96 © Mike Schroeder/Peter Arnold, Inc.

Printed in Canada

"In order to really enjoy a dog, one doesn't merely try to train him to be semi-human. The point of it is to open oneself to the possibility of becoming partly dog."

-Edward Hoagland

" We are drawn to dogs
because they are the
uninhibited creatures we
might be if we weren't
certain we knew better. "

-George Bird Evans

"Love is the answer, but sex raises some pretty good questions."

-Woody Allen

"I am extraordinarily patient provided I get my own way in the end.**"**

-Margaret Thatcher

“ The trouble with resisting temptation is that it may never come your way again. **”**

-Korman's Law

" My life is in the hands of any fool who makes me lose my temper. "

-Robert Benchley

" Forbid us something and that thing we desire. **"**

-Geoffrey Chaucer

> **"**The only way to deal with an unfree world is to become so absolutely free that your very existence is an act of rebellion.**"**
>
> - Albert Camus

"Every normal person must be tempted at times to spit upon their hands, hoist the black flag, and begin slitting throats."

-Lucanus

" We spend an enormous amount of time standing around in front of windows, just waiting. **"**

-Robert Benchley

" There is a charm about the forbidden that makes it unspeakably desirable. **"**

-Mark Twain

"If you know someone who tries
to drown their sorrows, you might
tell them sorrows know how to swim.**"**

-H. Jackson Browne, Jr.

> **"** That they may have a little peace, even the best dogs are compelled to snarl occasionally. **"**

-William Feather

"I like restraint—if it doesn't go too far."

-Mae West

"Most of us want to be delivered from temptation but would like it to stay in touch."

-Robert Orban

"Bite off more than you can chew
and then chew like hell."

-Peter Brock

"Nothing sharpens
sight like envy. **"**

-Thomas Fuller

"The sinning is the best part of repentance."

-Arab proverb

" Mischief, thou art afoot,
Take thou what course thou wilt.**"**

-William Shakespeare

"He that lives upon hope will die fasting.**"**

-Benjamin Franklin

"It's no use growing older
if you only learn new ways
of misbehaving yourself.**"**

-Hector Hugh Munro

" I have a tremendous amount
of anger, but I like to save
it—for my loved ones. "

-Susan Sullivan

" There are two types of
people in this world, good
and bad. The good sleep
better, but the bad seem to
enjoy the waking hours more. "

-Woody Allen

"But pleasures are like poppies spread;
You seize the flower, its bloom is shed."

-Robert Burns

"It is always easier to fight for one's principles than to live up to them."

-Alfred Adler

"We trifle when we set limits
to our desires, since
nature has set none."

-Christian Nevell Bovee

> **"** The avenues in my neighborhood are Pride, Covetousness and Lust; the cross streets are Anger, Gluttony, Envy and Sloth. I live over on Sloth, and the style on our street is to avoid the other thoroughfares. **"**
>
> -John Chancellor

"The devil doesn't know how to sing, only how to howl."

-Francis Thompson

If a small thing makes you angry, does that not indicate something about your size?

-Sydney J. Harris

"Guilt is God's way of letting you know that you're having too good a time."

-Dave Barry

> **"**I am not a glutton—I am an explorer of food.**"**
>
> -Erma Bombeck

"I have a right to my anger, and I don't want anyone telling me I shouldn't be, that it's not nice to be, and that something's wrong with me because I get angry.**"**

-Maxine Waters

> **"The only way to get rid of temptation is to yield to it."**
>
> -Oscar Wilde

"He that but looketh on a plate of ham and eggs to lust after it hath already committed breakfast in his heart."

-C.S. Lewis

"Guilt is the price we pay willingly for doing what we are going to do anyway.**"**

-Isabelle Holland

"A door is what a dog is perpetually
on the wrong side of."

-Ogden Nash

"Contentment is, after all,
refined indolence."

-Thomas C. Haliburton

"Anger is natural. You just have
to learn to hang out with it.**"**

-Tori Amos

"The more you let yourself go,
the less others let you go."

-Frederick Nietzsche

"Without the spice of guilt, sin cannot be fully savored."

-Alexander Chase

"A glass of desire is greater than a pitcher of talent."

-Andy Munthe

"They say the dog is man's best friend. I don't believe that. How many of your friends have you neutered?"

- Larry Reeb

"Every sin brings its punishment with it."

-Romanian proverb

" Quarrel? Nonsense; we have not quarreled. If one is not to get into a rage sometimes, what is the good of being friends? "

-George Eliot

"Guilt is present in the very hesitation, even though the deed not be committed."

-Cicero

"You will do foolish things,
but do them with enthusiasm.**"**

-Author Unknown